Stegosaurs

Roofed Dinosaurs

by Grace Hansen

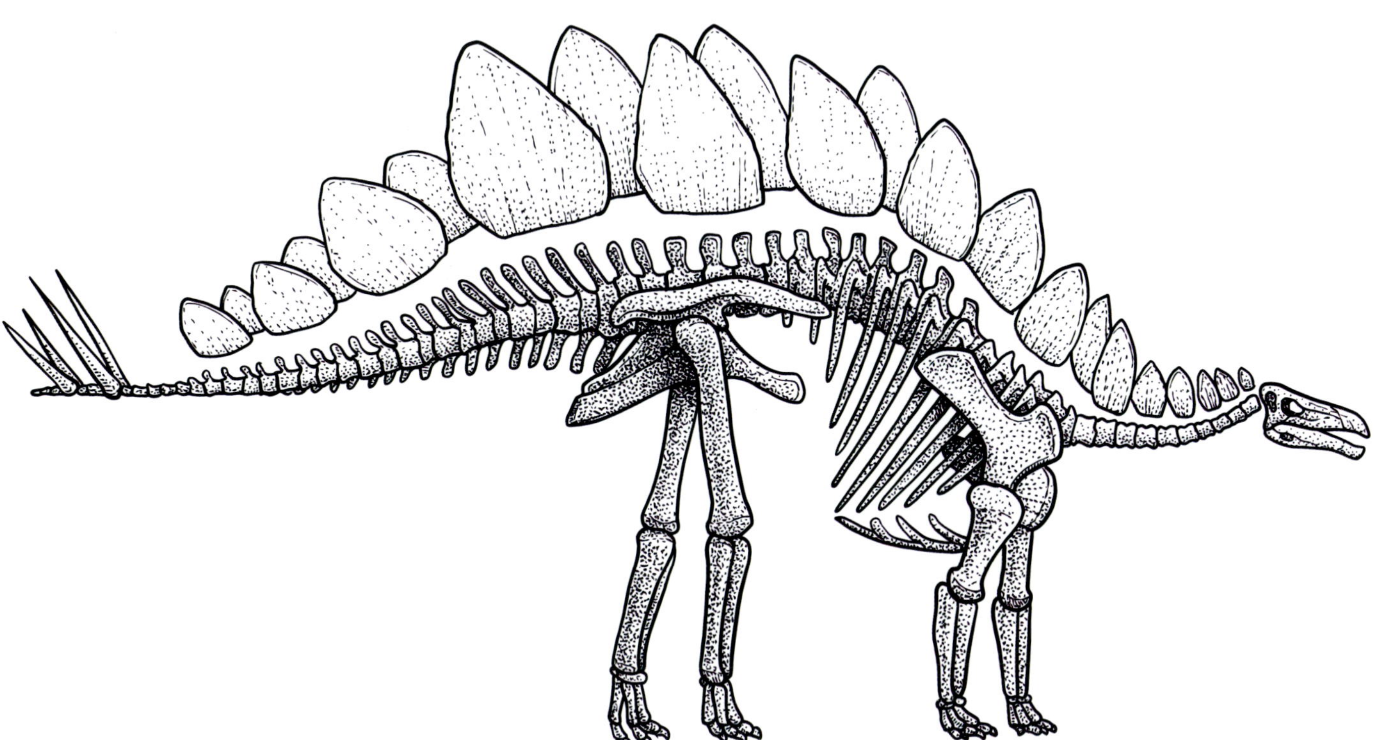

Abdo Kids Jumbo is an Imprint of Abdo Kids
abdobooks.com

abdobooks.com

Published by Abdo Kids, a division of ABDO, P.O. Box 398166, Minneapolis, Minnesota 55439.

Printed in the United States of America, North Mankato, Minnesota.

052025

092025

Photo Credits: Alamy, Getty Images, Science Source, Shutterstock

Production Contributors: Teddy Borth, Jennie Forsberg, Grace Hansen
Design Contributors: Victoria Bates, Candice Keimig

Library of Congress Control Number: 2024947618

Publisher's Cataloging-in-Publication Data

Names: Hansen, Grace, author.

Title: Stegosaurs: roofed dinosaurs / by Grace Hansen

Other Title: roofed dinosaurs

Description: Minneapolis, Minnesota : Abdo Kids, 2026 | Series: Dinosaur groups | Includes online resources and index.

Identifiers: ISBN 9798384905189 (lib. bdg.) | ISBN 9798384905882 (ebook) | ISBN 9798384906230 (read-to-me ebook)

Subjects: LCSH: Dinosaurs--Juvenile literature. | Prehistoric animals--Juvenile literature. | Animals, Fossil--Juvenile literature. | Paleontology--Juvenile literature.

Classification: DDC 567.90--dc23

Table of Contents

The Roofed Dinosaurs

Stegosaurs were a group of dinosaurs. They lived from the Jurassic to the Early Cretaceous Period. They were found throughout the world.

Jurassic
201 million
years ago
Cretaceous
145 million
years ago
Stegosaurs

Stegosaurs were large dinosaurs. They moved on four legs. Their front legs were much shorter than their back legs.

Stegosaurs are known for the double row of bony plates along their back and tail. The spikes at the end of the tail were likely used for defense.

Stegosaurs lived in wooded areas, open meadows, and river valleys. These places would have had lots of low-growing plants.

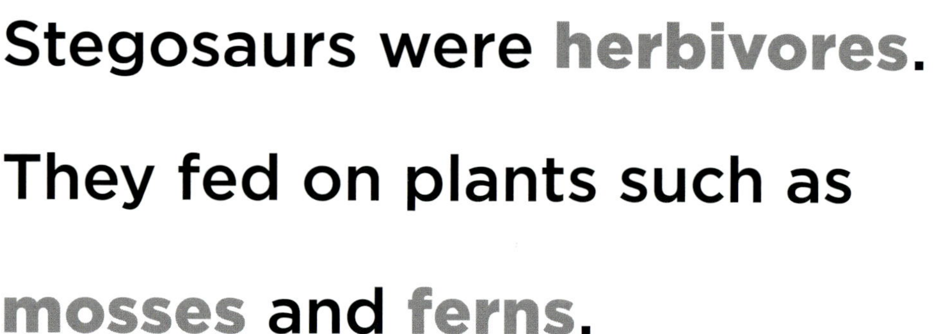

Stegosaurs were **herbivores**.

They fed on plants such as

mosses and **ferns**.

Huayangosaurus

Huayangosaurus was the smallest-known stegosaur. It had a row of spikes down its neck, back, and tail. It likely used its spikes for protection.

Middle Jurassic
Fossils found in
Asia
As long as a
small car
13.5 ft
(4 m) long
As heavy as a
polar bear
1,100 lbs
(500 kg)
Huayangosaurus

Kentrosaurus

Kentrosaurus was a close **relative** of *Stegosaurus*. The dinosaur had a very strong tail. It may have been able to swing its tail up to 22 miles per hour (35 kph)!

Late Jurassic
Fossils found in
Africa
As long as a
giraffe is tall
16 ft (5 m) long
As heavy as a
female and male bison
3,000 lbs
(1,360 kg)
Kentrosaurus

Dacentrurus

Dacentrurus was the first stegosaur ever discovered. It was also the largest! The first **fossils** were found in the town of Swindon in Wiltshire, England.

Late Jurassic
Fossils found in
Europe
As long as
half a bowling lane
30 ft (9 m) long
As heavy as an
RV
10,000 lbs
(4,500 kg)
Dacentrurus

Stegosaurus

Stegosaurus is the most well-known member of the stegosaur family. Its powerful spiked tail helped protect it from **predators** such as *Allosaurus*.

Common Stegosaur Features

Glossary

fern - a family of plants with large, green leaves shaped like feathers.

fossil - the remains or trace of a living animal or plant from a long time ago.

herbivore - an animal that only feeds on plants.

moss - a small, green plant without flowers that grows in soft, thick clumps.

predator - an animal that hunts other animals for food.

relative - an animal that is related to another animal.

Index